Better Athletics—Field (with Cross Country and Race Walking)

Better Athletics—Field
(with Cross Country and Race Walking)
(with 89 photographs and 9 diagrams)

by John Heaton

Principal Lecturer Physical Education
St. Paul's College Cheltenham.
British Amateur Athletics Board senior coach
Coach to Oxford University Athletics Club
(1960 to 1963)
County, Area, AAAs athlete

Kaye & Ward Ltd, London
in association with
Hicks, Smith & Sons. Australia and New Zealand

First published by
Kaye & Ward Ltd.
1973

ISBN 0 7182 0496 4

All enquiries and requests relevant to this title should
be sent to the publisher, Kaye & Ward Ltd, 21 New Street,
London EC2M 4NT, and not to the printer.

Filmset by Keyspools Ltd, Golborne, Lancs.
Printed in England by
Whitstable Litho, Straker Brothers Ltd.

Contents

Chapter 1   **Throwing**   **9**

Chapter 2   **Putting the Shot**   **15**

Chapter 3   **Throwing the Discus**   **27**

Chapter 4   **Throwing the Javelin**   **42**

Chapter 5   **Throwing the Hammer**   **53**

Chapter 6   **Cross Country Running**   **65**

Chapter 7   **Race Walking**   **75**

Chapter 8   **Indoor Athletics**   **84**

Chapter 9   **Choosing, Using and Looking After Personal Equipment**   **86**

Chapter 10   **Fitness and Testing**   **88**

Acknowledgements

I should like to express my gratitude to Mr Donald Bott of Winchcombe Street, Cheltenham, who took many of the photographs of the Cheltenham school children. My sincere thanks also go to Mr Tim Pike not only for taking photographs especially for the two volumes of *Better Athletics*, but also for allowing me to select from his vast library of athletic action photographs.

Thanks to the secretary of the English Schools Athletics Association for the photographs of the Nationals, and also to the boys from Elmfield School, Cheltenham Grammar School and Malvern College, to the students of St Pauls College, Cheltenham, and the girls and boys of Monkscroft School, Cheltenham, who all co-operated magnificently by acting as subjects for some of the photographs.

I freely acknowledge the debt I owe to all the students, teachers, coaches and athletes who, over my years in athletics, have taught me a great deal and are indirectly contributing to these books.

Finally, thanks to my wife and family who were always ready with helpful suggestions and lots of encouragement.

Cheltenham   John Heaton

Foreword

Teaching athletics is a difficult business—it requires enormous patience, cunning psychology and above all a genuine love for the sport. These qualities John Heaton has in giant measure—as I found to my great advantage when he coached me at Oxford. By profession a lecturer in Physical Education at last he has the chance to combine his teaching skills with his enormous experience of athletics to all our benefits.

Adrian Metcalfe,
Silver Medallist Olympic Games
London Week End Television

Introduction

This book and its companion volume have been written to help boys and girls learn about athletics through enjoyment by taking part and so improving performances.

It is easy to be put off by failure resulting from trying to emulate all that top-class athletes do, and it can make you give up trying when you compare the times and speeds at which these people run and the distances they jump with your own.

What you should be concerned with is your own improvement and the question you should keep asking yourself is 'How far have I come?' Though work is necessary in order to achieve success it can be enjoyable. If you prepare work-outs yourself and with others using these books it will all be more interesting.

You will enjoy trying out what John Heaton has suggested in the text. He has vast experience as a top-class athlete, a teacher, a lecturer in Physical Education, and an Amateur Athletics Association staff coach and he has put his knowledge into practice in the coaching of athletics at all levels.

I consider the author to be one of the greatest teachers of athletics I have ever met.

Bill Marlow,
BAAB National Coach Midland Counties

1. THROWING

There is little doubt about the increasing interest in Field Throwing Events. They are well covered by television, and producers now make sure that the cameramen turn their attention not only to the track, but also to pits and heaps of soft landing material, as well as the run ups, and particularly to cement circles, wire cages, and marked arcs and areas used in the various throwing events.

These events can be dangerous if safety precautions are not taken, not only when competing but also when practising. Here are a few points for you to think about when you compete and practise.

1. Always *carry* your implement safely (e.g. javelin upright) and do not swing your hammer about, or do pretend throws. There may be other people quite near.

1. These young athletes carry their implements safely over to the throwing area.

2. Novice discus throwers throwing from a standing position behind a line. No-one fetches the discus until all have thrown. A leader or coach says when they must go. The same would apply in shot, javelin and hammer but with appropriate spacing.

   2. When you are with a group and practising, use a marked line or area to throw from, and throw in one known direction only.

   3. Throwing to each other is a bad way to practise, so do not do it: it is dangerous.

   4. Make sure you do not go to pick up your implement until everyone else has thrown.

   5. *Neither judges, stewards nor athletes should throw implements back to competitors under any circumstances.*

   6. Keep a cloth handy for drying wet or moist implements.

The Rules of Competition state quite clearly that, in order to avoid accidents,

   1. throwing areas should be roped off and safety nets used;

2. safety areas covering the landing areas should be roped off and patrolled by officials during competitions;
3. competitors must be given instructions that even during practice, implements must be thrown only from the circles or sector line, or in the immediate vicinity thereof, and must be returned, during practice or competition, by hand and not thrown back to the starting area.

The referee, or other appropriate official, shall disqualify from competition in the event any athlete who wilfully disobeys the above instructions after having his attention drawn to them.

It is also recommended that each throw is signalled just before it is made, whether in practice or in competition. This signal is often given with a hooter or horn. Next time you go to a meeting, watch and listen.

Don't be put off from taking up throwing events. You have probably thrown a cricket ball and I am sure that you must have tried skimming stones over the surface of the sea or a lake. You have probably tried to put some heavy object further than someone else. From these, and other similar sorts of activities have come the throwing events. When you start throwing, don't worry about the restricting areas used in competitions. Throw first and then adapt to the lines and circles.

For boys and girls there are particular weights and measurements for the implements used in competition laid down by the English Schools Athletic Association. The throwing areas and sectors are the same for each age group.

Shot

	Boys	*Girls*
Junior (Under 15)	4·00 kgs	3·25 kgs
Intermediate (Over 15 Under 17)	5·00 kgs	4·00 kgs
Senior (Over 17 Under 20)	6·25 kgs	4·00 kgs
Hammer		
Junior	4·00 kgs	—
Intermediate	5·00 kgs	—
Senior	6·25 kgs	—

3. Different discus sizes. Reading left to right, ladies competition, rubber practice, junior and senior competition sizes. Always use throwing implements you can really manage in the early learning stages.

Discus

	Weight	*Boys* Thickness at Centre	Diameter
Juniors	1·25 kgs	37 mm/39 mm	180 mm/182 mm
Intermediate	1·5 kgs	37 mm/42 mm	200 mm/205 mm
Seniors	1·75 kgs	41 mm/43 mm	210 mm/212 mm

	Weight	*Girls* Thickness at Centre	Diameter
Juniors Intermediate } Seniors	1·00 kg	37 mm/39 mm	180 mm/182 mm

Javelin

	Minimum length	Maximum length	Distance from point to C. of Gravity	Minimum weight
Junior *Boys* and all *Girls*	220 cm	230 cm	80 cm/95 cm	600 gms
Intermediate *Boys*	230 cm	240 cm	83 cm/99 cm	700 gms
Senior *Boys*	260 cm	270 cm	90 cm/110 cm	800 gms

A Few General Points from The Rules of Competition:

1. There are throwing arcs with sectors in which the implements must land as follows: 45 degrees for the hammer, discus and shot whilst the javelin must land within a 28-degree sector.
2. The circle for the discus is 2·5 metres in diameter, and for the shot and hammer 2·135 metres. The javelin is thrown from a corridor 4 metres wide, behind an arc.
3. A white line shall be drawn across the circles dividing them into rear and front halves and extending 75 cms outside. All circle event competitors must retire after their attempts from the rear half of the circle. The javelin thrower must stay behind the arc and line.
4. All lines, circles and sectors are 'foul' territory except on the vertical inside edge of things like the stop board.
5. The winner is the person who throws the furthest. When there is a tie, the tying competitor with the next best throw is the winner.
6. Unless the mark first made by the implement on landing is inside the sector lines, the throw does not count.

You will notice that I have not mentioned standards at this stage. It is important that you enjoy your throwing and jumping and running, and are not put off by apparently being so far behind some laid down standard or by seeing and hearing about international athletes breaking records. In the early stages the performance you should be competing to improve is your own.

There is also pleasure to be had from flighting the discus, spearing targets with the javelin, and heaving the shot. Hitting targets and acquiring new skills can be most rewarding. Remember also that you do not necessarily grow in size at the same rate as your friend or others of the same age and so you should make sure that your implement is the most suitable size for you. Remember that equipment which is too small and light can be as much of a handicap as that which is too big and heavy.

You cannot learn to throw just by reading a book and looking at pictures. You have to go out and try, using the time you are out with equipment to have some sort of competition, to think about the move-

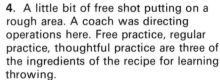

4. A little bit of free shot putting on a rough area. A coach was directing operations here. Free practice, regular practice, thoughtful practice are three of the ingredients of the recipe for learning throwing.

5. Spearing targets from behind a line makes an interesting activity. Judging by the results in this photograph it's not quite as easy as it looks for these first time throwers.
The idea of target practices can be applied to other events.

ments you are doing and to get help from someone who is watching by asking them if they would look for some particular feature of your technique. Afterwards you should read about the event and talk over what you are trying to do.

That is why at least some of your athletics, apart from competition, ought to be done in the company of someone else. Mutual discussion and observation can make the activities more interesting and profitable.

In the chapters which follow I have tried to suggest activities for you to do, ideas you can work on and things you can think about when practising the events. Also included are points which an observer or a coach could look for, particularly during your practice times. You can also take note of these when you watch other people perform.

14

2. PUTTING THE SHOT

Have you ever had to carry a stone of potatoes? The men at the Olympics are required to put a shot which weighs two pounds more than that. In metric measurements, the shot weights 7·25 kgs. But you will not be competing with anything quite as heavy as that just yet.

SOME FUNDAMENTALS ABOUT PUTTING

The rules require that the shot is *pushed* from the shoulder, not thrown. This means that the shot must never get behind the elbow of the throwing arm and it must remain in contact with the shoulder during any pre-liminary movements.

Basically, you use the strongest muscles, which are in the legs and body, as well as the weight of your body, to start the heavy shot moving and then bring in the muscles of the arm and shoulder which move the arms quickly to accelerate the already moving weight.

Strong legs and trunk muscles are just as important as strong arms for the field event performers.

The shot cannot go any faster than you are moving and does not speed up when it leaves your hand, so your fastest movements come just as the implement leaves. It should leave at an angle of almost 40 degrees.

WAYS OF PUTTING THE SHOT

There are a number of styles, some of which are named after the people who first used them. Remember that although these styles were good for them, they might not all suit you. They all involve a low hop across the

6. *(far left)* The effort of applying full force from a firm base can be seen as Mary Peters puts the shot indoors at Cosford.

7. *(left)* The shot has been thrust away but she has stayed in the circle partly by changing her feet about. This is called the reverse.

shot put circle, which is 2·135 metres in diameter, and end in a putting position with the front foot near the stop board and the rear foot just past the centre of the circle.

The speed and force of actually putting the implement would cause any athlete to fall out of the circle and be disqualified unless he took action, but this is avoided by means of a quick foot change after the shot has gone, and bending of the legs.

LEARNING TO PUT

If you have not done any shot putting before, then get used to the activity of heaving a weight by trying different ways of sending the weight away from you. Do not worry about a circle at first. Learn the basics and then accommodate to the circle. Here are some methods, and I have no doubt you could invent others. Practise competitively and with someone else helping, first freely, then from behind the line.

(a) Two handed throws from between the legs.

16

(b) One handed throws.

(c) Throw under arm.

(d) Shot put type movement after a run up.

(e) If you have thrown a discus, try putting from the shoulder after a discus turn.

Playing about in different ways like this will get you used to the weight of the implement. Mark targets on the ground and try to reach them. Throw for height and distance. Mark a line to put or throw from and have a competition. In order to save measuring each attempt, mark the landing area at, say, metre intervals. You could use a tin lid to mark your attempts. Not only does it become a useful target but it does enable you to see progress.

8. Two boys have free practice projecting the shot in a two-handed throwing competition.

9. Here the boys are moving up to a line to do a single-handed put. Note the pegs to mark the putting point for each competitor.

17

Sometimes the trajectory or angle of flight is too shallow so use, say, a high jump bar at about 45 degrees so that you can get an idea of what the angle is like. (See photograph 15.)

Put a rope across the high jump stands and try throwing the shot over, then try putting it over.

When you are feeling more at home with the weight, begin to build up a technique. At various times the following points should be noted.

10 and 11. Two shot putters, one a novice, the other, on the right, Geoff Capes the British record holder. Notice how the stronger Capes has the shot high on his fingers and thumb.

HOLDING THE SHOT

Look at the photographs. There are a number of ways of letting the shot come to rest in your hand before putting. You have already used one or other method. The point to remember is that if you are not strong enough in the fingers, the shot must be held a little nearer the palm. Ultimately, your aim is to be able to put with the shot resting at the base of the fingers. The thumb and little finger just support at the sides.

12. Preparing to put is important. The athlete is beginning to settle for the put. He has adjusted the shot in his fingers, put his feet right but does not appear to be concentrating yet.

13. From the upright position the putter has moved to bend his knees and Geoff Capes is seen just before driving across the circle. To bend your leg as much as this you have to be strong, so don't copy too closely unless you can cope.

A FEW FUNDAMENTALS FOR THE STANDING PUT

When you get to the point where you are beginning to think of really being a shot putter, it is as well to do some putting without any movement across the circle. This will enable you to think about one or two fundamentals. You should be aware of some of these yourself but it is as well if someone standing about 4 metres away helps you.

The coach should stand at the side or behind you. Here are the points he should look for and you should think about when doing the standing put:

The Legs and Feet (for a right-handed person. Reverse for left-hander.)
 (a) Foot positions as in the diagram.
 (b) The knees are bent with the weight mainly over the right foot at the start. The right knee should be bent more than the left.
 (c) The toes of the left foot only on the ground at the start.
 (d) Leg drive is upward as well as forward through the hips.

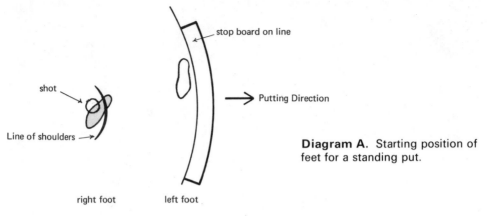

shot

Line of shoulders →

stop board on line

→ Putting Direction

Diagram A. Starting position of feet for a standing put.

right foot   left foot

Hands and Arms

(i) The non-putting arm is important as it affects the put.

    (a) It should first be bent across the body.

    (b) It should be brought round rapidly as if hitting with the back of the upper arm.

    (c) It should be kept up high, as this helps to stabilize the left shoulder and left side round which you are pivoting.

    (d) The hand should be relaxed.

(ii) The putting arm.

    (a) The elbow should be out and away from the side.

    (b) The shot should be held in the neck.

    (c) The arm should not begin to apply its force until the shoulder and body have started the shot on its way. Watch for this.

    (d) The arm and hand should keep contact with the shot for as long as possible by following through and reaching after the shot has gone.

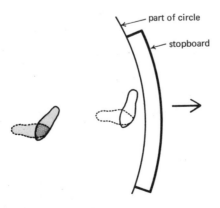

part of circle

stopboard

Diagram B. Dotted lines show the position the feet move through when a put is being made. Solid line=starting position.

14. A standing put. The feet are in a fairly useful position, though the hips have perhaps not been thrust forward enough. The left arm has dropped and so has the shoulder. As with most beginners, not enough body weight has gone into the put and the left side is not fixed. However, full marks for effort.

15. By using a pole vault at about 45° the putter gets an idea of the flight path. A high jump bar held across acts as a target to put over and improve projection. Up and out is the thinking here.

16. If you really want to know what it is like to drive across the circle then look at Geoff Capes. Can you see how he is looking back and curling his arm and shoulders round the shot ready for the explosive unwind a moment or two later?

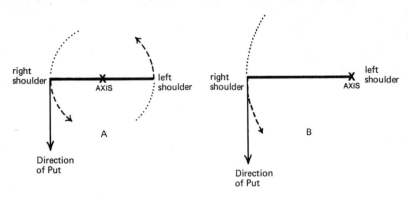

Diagram C. This shows how quite a difference results from changing the part of the body you rotate round. Provided the speed at each axis is the same then the right shoulder holding the shot moves faster.

The Shoulders

   (a) At this point in the shot put they will be rotating with the left shoulder and side as the pivot, not the spine.

   (b) The left shoulder relative to a point on the ground will go forward.

   (c) It is important that the left shoulder is kept high.

THE STANDING PUT

The put is made by driving with the legs, through the hips, which turn first, followed by the shoulders, and then the arm pushes. These movements run one into the other and herein lies the difficulty. So, whether helping or performing, questions to which you have to answer 'Yes' if technique is good include the following.

Was the movement:

   (i) a continuous one; legs, hips, trunk, shoulder, arm-hand sequence?

   (ii) one which enabled force to be applied to the shot for as long as possible?

   (iii) initiated by the legs and hips, carried on by the body and completed by the arms and hands?

   (iv) over as great a distance as possible?

   (v) an explosive movement?

   (vi) thought of as an upward and outward push and punch with a trunk twist?

   (vii) one in which you started with the head and shoulders facing backwards as on landing but with the hips tending to turn towards the front ready to be thrust further forward.

22

17. *(left)* Having landed in the putting position, the drive has been from the right leg with the hip thrusting early. Note that the arm has not yet made much contribution. What a good firm braced left side and high shoulder.

18. *(right)* Bill Fielder also shows how to keep a firm left side, use the legs and thrust the shot out high. He is already following the shot and his right leg is coming forward presently to check forward movement.

19. *(left)* This photograph of a Lancashire Junior Champion shows the hips coming round as the left leg is braced to allow him to pivot. The drive from the right leg has finished.

20. *(right)* A terrific drive into the shot with the shoulders really turning to punch the implement away.

PUTTING AFTER MOVING ACROSS THE CIRCLE

The preliminary movements before the actual put help to build up momentum in the shot. There are a number of ways of doing this. Usually, the learner begins by a run or step across the 2·135-metre diameter circle, others do a sideways hop or glide. If you are interested and keen enough and have time to practise the backward hop, it is a useful method. When you are strong enough it can lead easily into the O'Brien style which most senior athletes use. If you are not very big, you might have to start your glide nearer the centre of the circle in order to get across to the stop board. Go out and try the movements in photograph 21.

21. First attempts at moving before putting. The boy furthest away is mainly using the arm, the boy in the centre is very open whilst the boy nearest the camera has not really turned his hip but he has used his shoulders to advantage. The important thing, however, is that these boys are having a go.

24

Backward Glide or Low Hop Method (right-handed putter)

(a) Stand at the rear of the circle, or near the rear if you are not big enough to use the whole circle, with your back to the direction in which you wish to put. Hold the shot in your shoulder, with the left arm raised and across the chest.

(b) With the shot remaining in the shoulder, bend forward and lift the left leg back.

(c) By bringing the left leg in, flexing it, you will begin to move towards the centre of the circle.

(d) By a rapid straightening of the left leg and a push with the right leg, you will hop or 'low glide' across the circle.

(e) As the right foot lands in or near the middle of the circle, the left foot is brought down near the stop board and the put is begun as described in the section on the Standing Put.

You must make sure that:

(a) the hop is low with the right leg landing at right angles to the direction of the throw just before the left;

(b) you look backwards and downwards until you land;

(c) the shot stays at your shoulder with the left arm across the chest during the hop;

(d) the hop is in a line with the direction of the throw;

(e) the left leg has been thrust down before the accelerating, twisting upward and outward trunk action begins;

(f) the left shoulder is kept up by keeping the left arm up as the put is made;

(g) the hips come round as you land but the head and shoulders remain facing backwards. This gives a torque or twist effect which is taken up as the actual putting takes place;

(h) the legs have been really used to add impetus to the shot, i.e. the knees are extended, as the shoulders come round and arm thrust is added;

(i) when pushing the shot you have contact with the ground until the shot has left your hand.

25

You will find that when you push hard at the shot, punching with your arm and reaching out after it, you will be falling out of the circle over the stop board. Avoid this by a quick jump change of leg positions, called a 'reverse'. You push off with your left leg and land on a bent right leg with the outside of the right foot against the inside of the stop board. Most people do not need to be taught this.

STANDARDS
To help you judge how well you are getting on, here are some targets which the ESAA have decided on.

Qualifying standards for entry to the 1972 Nationals:

Shot

	Boys		Girls	
Junior	(4 kgs)	11·75 metres	(3·25 kgs)	9·60 metres
Intermediate	(5 kgs)	13·53 metres	(4 kgs)	9·80 metres
Senior	(6·25 kgs)	13·56 metres	(4 kgs)	10·31 metres

3. THROWING THE DISCUS

The classical statue of the Discus Thrower by Myron has long been a symbol of athletic prowess, physical fitness and sporting achievement. Perhaps that is why many people have been inspired to take up the event.

To make the discus skim from the hand and flight its way streamlined through the air is a satisfying achievement in itself, and to improve distance only adds to the pleasure.

Early success is not easily come by because you do not really *throw* the discus. You sling it with your hand on top, and at first you feel that the thing is going to drop from your hand before you can project it, so insecure does it feel.

It follows therefore that before you can start doing those turns in the discus circle, you should have lots of practice at flighting the discus by throwing from more or less a standing position. Think of the number of times you have perhaps kicked a football or hit a ball. When you have thrown a discus as many times as that, you should be quite a proficient thrower.

Getting the discus to fly through the air properly is the first task.

Next, you have to add more velocity or speed to the implement.

The distance you throw results from a combination of three things:

(a) The speed of the discus when you let it go.
(b) The angle at which it leaves; e.g. throw it straight up and it will drop at your feet, throw it horizontally and it lands 'too soon'.
(c) The way in which the implement flies through the air. That is whether it spins or not and whether it flies with its edge leading or whether it looks like a full moon gradually receding. This is called its 'attitude'.

22. Getting in lots of throwing practice. Note the supply of discoi ready for further attempts. Having the next missile handy saves a walk after each throw. Note that this practice discus circle is off the track and in an area of rough ground where throwing can be practised freely.

LEARNING TO THROW
1. General Points

First of all, make sure you have a discus which is of manageable size. Start with a small one.

If you are keen and can get hold of half a dozen discoi or you are able to throw one discus many times into a net, you can get in much more practice than if you have to take turns, fetch the discus after each throw and wait around.

The important thing when learning is to get in lots of actual throwing, thinking carefully about what you are doing and with a friend to watch for points of technique.

Before going any further, I must remind you here about those safety factors by asking you to:

(a) make sure you are using a designated throwing area;
(b) throw one way only;
(c) remember that if you are in a group, throw only when a leader signals and do not run out to retrieve until it is safe to do so. Usually this is on a signal when all the discs have been thrown.

In order to get in a lot of practice it seems best to go alone, in pairs or with a group of not more than four and have about a dozen implements. Take it in turns to throw. Any non-throwers must stand a few yards back from the throwing line or circle.

23. *(left)* How to first position the discus in the hand is shown in the bottom picture. The middle and upper picture show how the discus leaves the hand.

24. *(above)* A group, having got the hold correct, practise swinging the discus in various arcs. Eventually they should feel more comfortable about the discus staying in the hand and do it like Rosemary Payne in the next photograph.

2. Basic Techniques (right-handed thrower)

Grip or Hold

Unless you have the correct 'hold' on the discus you will not make much progress and will fall into bad habits which could prevent success, and you will be dissatisfied.

(a) First, put the discus on the palm of the throwing hand—in this case, the right hand. Palm uppermost.

25. Rosemary Payne, British Champion and record holder, prior to throwing. Look at her position at the rear of the circle, the way that the discus is parallel to the ground and the left and right shoulders almost level.

(b) Let the ends of the fingers just come over the edge of the discus—
don't grip round the rim. The line of your index finger should pass
almost through the centre plate of the discus.

(c) Now turn your hand over, preventing the discus from falling down
by using the left hand, and stretch out your arm at shoulder
level (see photograph 23). This is how the discus is positioned in
the hand prior to throwing.

Practising Holding, Swinging and Spinning

1. With your hand at your side, let the discus rest on the finger tips.
Now swing your arm backwards and forwards, gradually increasing
the range (see photograph 24). This will enable you to feel the discus
pressing on the finger tips.

2. Change to swinging in an arc across the front of the body, using
the left hand at the end of each swing to the front to stop the
implement from dropping. Try to keep the right hand parallel to
the ground. Do not have your thumb higher than your little finger,
except when the discus is swung back.

3. With the discus in the hand and the arm to the side, spin the discus
clockwise, first by letting the weight of the discus move over on to
your (index) finger, then by bending quickly at the elbow and
throwing the discus slightly upward.

4. Place the discus on the upturned palm of your left hand, held out
in front of the right shoulder. Put your right hand on top in a correct
'grip' position. Now, by swinging the right arm across, push the
discus away using the index finger as the last point of contact. You
almost squeeze the discus away as you push. This will give you an
idea of the position of the right hand with its palm down and at
shoulder height when the discus leaves. You should also feel how
the hand comes across the back of the discus at delivery with the
index finger making contact.

5. Freely practise any swings of the right arm whilst holding the
discus. These will enable you to become confident that the discus
will not fall.

26. *(left)* The Midlands Women's Discus Championship. Mrs Payne shows how legs should drive, hips thrust and the shoulders come round before the discus arm. There is also a firm left side and base to throw from. Get someone to look for these in your throws.

27 *(right)* An English schoolboy shows a good upright position after the discus has gone. No bending to the left here. Standing throws should feature these points.

6. Start by holding the discus high overhead with left and right hand in contact, then swing in a horizontal arc.

7. Practise a 'scything' movement of swinging the discus. This means a swing which is parallel to the ground, with the legs bent. Use the left hand to support the discus when it comes to the left front and stops.

8. As for 7, but move forward as a man does when he scythes a field. This will enable you to think of putting your body weight into the movement before the arm comes round.

9. Increase the body turn to give a greater range of movement, particularly the turn backwards.

Release and Standing Throw

1. The 'scything' movements with the bent legs and body and arm turning are continued. The palm is always on top and the discus is brought round parallel to the ground and at shoulder height for two or three swings. On, say, the third 'scythe' or swing, release the discus as you turn round and the arm is catching up with the

shoulders. Push the discus off with your index finger. The discus trajectory will be low but the implement should flight well.

2. As above, but use the legs to give more power and lift. That is to say, as you are swinging the arm round your legs, stretch thus adding lift.

3. Try to imagine that there is a high shelf about 1·3 metres in front of you and up at about 3 metres. As you come round to sling, try to imagine that you are putting the discus flat on to the shelf. When it is on its way you continue to reach after it as though wishing to take it down again. Do this at a moderate or slow speed, thinking of the position or attitude of the discus in the air as the important factor. The discus should land on the ground about 3·3 metres away or even less. Turn your chest and right shoulder into the movement first before the arm comes round. Gradually increase effort and distance.

4. Put your feet in line with the direction of throw except that the left (front) leg will be slightly to the left to allow the hips to turn and face the direction of throw. Now swing or sling with increasing effort following the scything movements (diagram of foot position).

5. Try right from the start to leave the throwing arm behind so that it is rather like a whip-lash coming after the stock has moved. The body, particularly the right leg and hips, drive round first before the arm comes round. The left shoulder and arm finish high (see photograph 25).

6. Try slinging from a standing position by first standing with both feet together then, as the discus is taken back, stepping back with your weight over the right leg which immediately straightens with a vigorous movement to transfer weight forwards on to the left leg, and pushing the hips and body round to 'free' the throwing arm which comes later but fast to 'catch up'. Delivery is at shoulder level.

7. Once you feel able to get a reasonable flight with a moderate effort (nothing will have been done with 100 per cent power but will have

been performed with controlled effort), you can begin to increase the effort, aiming at this stage to get a good flight of the discus and a 45-degree release angle. Try landing the discus on to targets of some sort.

8. Hold a jumping lath at 45 degrees from shoulder height to give you an idea of the flight path.
9. Do some measuring of standing throws and record them.

28. *(left)* Guy Dirkin (Lancs.) E.S.A.A. Senior Boys Discus Champion shows a good delivery position. Just look how those hips and legs have contributed by full extension.

29. *(right)* Fiona Melnik in the middle of throwing a world record in the European Championships at Helsinki. Look how she is running into her throw and also how her body weight is going in the direction she wants to throw. The discus is coming last and her turning seems to be made easier and therefore faster by keeping her arm with the discus fairly near the body.

Improving the Throw (Standing)

Find someone to watch you throw and get them to look at one feature only as each attempt is made. Here are some things they can look for.

The observer should see that:

(a) the feet are in the right position before, during and after throwing;
(b) the discus is brought round for the throw in a line with the shoulders;

(c) the correct spin of the discus on release is achieved. This means that the hand comes across the 'back' of the discus. It will be clockwise for a right-hander;

(d) the left shoulder is held up high;

(e) the hips and chest lead the movement;

(f) the throwing arm does not race round;

(g) the leg drive is made full use of;

(h) the explosive-effort comes at the end;

(i) the movement is a controlled accelerating one with the fastest movement at the end;

(j) the thrower is in contact with the ground when the throw is made;

(k) the jump reverse comes after the discus has left;

(l) the hips and chest come round first with a trailing throwing arm.

DISCUS TURNS

For some aspirants the standing throw will produce longer throws than those they do with a turn, but full use made of the circle by some form of turn will eventually produce longer throws.

$1\frac{1}{2}$ or $1\frac{3}{4}$ accelerating turns before the discus is projected will give you the time and distance required to build up speed.

LEARNING THE $1\frac{3}{4}$ TURN

Start with your back towards the direction in which you wish to throw. Stand with feet astride the direction-of-throw line. Swing the discus back and, as it reaches the furthermost point, start to turn using the left foot as a pivot. As your right leg comes round, drive across the circle putting the right foot down at the centre after a low 'bound'. As the right foot comes down on the circle the left leg comes round and is placed quickly in position to the left of the throwing line and near the front of the circle. Body and arm are trailing this movement and as the left foot touches at the front, the right leg drives forwards and upwards, pushing the hips round, and the movement is as for the standing throw.

This turning is a difficult movement to control and should only be attempted at a speed well within your capacity.

30. Strap discus can be used when learning turns. You can concentrate on the leg movements without worrying about dropping the discus. Use mainly for early practice.

Diagram D. A $1\frac{1}{2}$ to $1\frac{3}{4}$ discus turn.

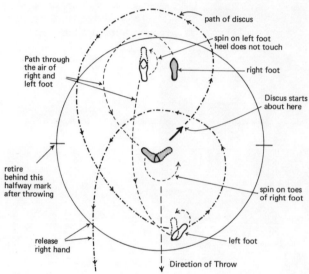

path of discus

spin on left foot
heel does not touch

right foot

Path through
the air of
right and
left foot

Discus starts
about here

retire
behind this
halfway mark
after throwing

spin on toes
of right foot

release
right hand

left foot

Direction of Throw

31 and 32. These boys and girls are learning the turn with and without a discus. There is no release of the implement. The lines on the games field are used as the direction throwing line. Lines also help in checking on foot placements as well as providing a target for the feet.

Hints for Beginners

1. At the start of the turn your knees should be bent with the body weight over the balls of the feet. Hips, knees and ankles are flexed almost at right angles (see photograph 33). The key to a good turn is balance at the start. So begin the turn with your weight controlled over the left foot.

33. A young athlete starts his movement across the circle. Weight on left foot, a fair degree of balance, bent knees, level shoulders and head leading are features to note.

2. As you go in to the turn, your body weight is really moving backwards towards the front of the circle (see photograph 33).
3. The movement is one in which your weight should move along the throwing line.
4. When your right foot comes to the ground after the low drive across the circle, it is turned in so that it is anticipating the turn.
5. Begin the whole movement slowly and get the speed after the left

foot has landed and you are in a throwing position. A common fault is to rush into the turn like a sprinter moving on the gun.

6. Let the head lead the movement round, with the legs and hips also leading the arm.

7. Do not start your turn by moving the left foot back. Use the whole circle.

8. It is useful to practise turning without a discus, using a line to 'travel' along (see photograph 32).

34. *(left)* John Turton, Essex Senior Boys who threw 46·32 metres begins his drive across the circle. Look at the almost sprint position of the legs. Cover up the top half of the picture and you will see what is meant. Note the safety net on this and other competition photographs.

35. *(right)* John Watts of the Royal Marines in a vest he has exchanged throwing 59·70 metres at Leicester. Just look at that lean into the throw and the determination-to-do-well look. Note the trailing arm, a good feature.

9. If you have done a good discus turn you will find yourself finishing without breaking away to your left. You will feel that your body weight is going after the discus.

10. If you are 'following through' you can avoid falling out of the circle by doing a reverse, which means jumping and changing your legs about.

11. Do not let the discus go up and down as you turn. Keep it steady.

12. As you begin the turn and your weight is falling towards the front of the circle but is still on the left foot, look for the place where your right foot is going to be placed. That is about the centre spot.

37. *(below)* A quick left foot plant is featured by Guy Dirkin in the Junior Championships at Wolverhampton. It comes immediately after the right foot has landed. The left leg is beginning to be braced. At this point weight is over the right foot and he is about to twist and drive into the throw with hips leading.

36. *(above)* Guy Dirkin of Lancashire shows a good body and hip lead so that the right foot can come down quickly at the centre. Low flight and turn are clearly demonstrated here coming after the left leg drive. Look how the discus has been left behind.

38

13. In the final phase the left arm and shoulder should be kept high. The left side makes a firm braced axis round which the final sling is made.

14. Do not try to get a better release angle by first lowering the discus and throwing it upwards. Use your legs to get lift as the final part of the turn is made.

TRAINING

After a general warm-up period of exercises and general running, go into some turning and throwing practice for about half an hour or two twenty-minute sessions. These can take the form of throws done in a number of ways, e.g.:

(a) in groups of three or six done as a competition;

(b) six throws with increasing range;

(c) a throwing competition against an opponent;

(d) throwing into a net a fixed number of times in a fixed period of time;

(e) rapid throwing into a net or out into the field if you have enough discoi, e.g. greatest number you can throw in two minutes without losing too much technique.

Activities (d) and (e) are a sort of pressure training and can lead to loss of technique. Use them wisely.

Sometimes a light shot can be slung instead of a discus.

During your practices you must at some point have your mind on some specific point of technique. Here are some of the things you might think about:

(a) Foot positioning.

(b) Timing of the turn.

(c) Arm position relative to the body during the turn.

(d) Relaxation of the throwing arm.

(e) Timing of movements with maximum speed and effort at the end.

(f) Making full use of the circle.

(g) Keeping the left arm and shoulder high.

(h) Getting the left leg into position early, and use of the legs generally.

(i) Completing the throw whilst in contact with the ground.

(j) Angle of release and attitude of discus.

(k) The follow through, reaching out after the discus and then reversing the feet with a jump.

Once you have achieved something like a turn, only practice of the full turn is really useful. You may use a part turn just to feel a position but full turns should be done more often than not.

You should practise all the year round if you make this your event. It might mean practising on a cold day. Use a pail of hot water to warm up the discus and your hands. Don't forget a towel.

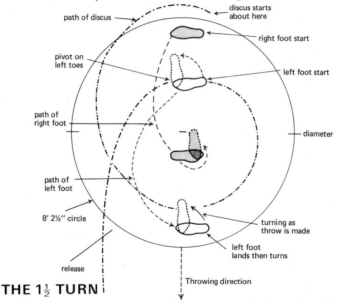

Diagram E. Foot movements and path of discus in a $1\frac{1}{4}$ turn discus throw.

THE $1\frac{1}{2}$ TURN

If the $1\frac{3}{4}$ turn is too much to start with, knock off a quarter and do $1\frac{1}{2}$ turns. This means starting with your left side facing the direction of throw, your right foot at the back of the circle and your left foot about two feet away. The turn is then as for the $1\frac{3}{4}$ turn but there is not the body torque or twist and control is easier.

The fundamentals and hints apply just the same and many beginners will find it useful to start with a $1\frac{1}{2}$ turn and work up, but this is not always the case.

For the record. The Olympic Record is 64·78 metres and the National Qualifying Standards (1972) are:

Discus

	Boys	Girls
Junior	36·20 metres	26.50 metres
Intermediate	38·32 metres	30·40 metres
Senior	39·22 metres	32·70 metres

At a schools meeting the standard expected would be

		Boys	Girls
Junior	Under 13	24·40 metres	16·00 metres
	Under 14	28·44 metres	18·00 metres
	Under 15	30·16 metres	21·10 metres
Intermediate	Under 16	27·56 metres	23·50 metres
	Under 17	30·80 metres	24·70 metres
Senior	Under 18	25·80 metres	25·60 metres
	Under 19	30·20 metres	26·20 metres
	Under 20	32·54 metres	26·70 metres

38. Look at the way the discus is leaving the hand, the effort and concentration, and the use made of the legs, and you will get a good idea of what to do.

4. THROWING THE JAVELIN

Throwing a javelin is not an easy activity initially and it might be as well to try throwing a cricket ball or tennis ball first to discover how you fare. It requires a jerking movement after leading with the elbow. If you can throw a ball reasonably well you should be able to throw a javelin.

In athletics there are no actual targets to throw at but only personal targets of achievement to aim for, in the form of distance thrown. For a throw to be recorded all you have to do is to throw from a marked area and make the javelin land point first. It does not need to stick in but just make a mark.

Before we go any further, as javelins are pointed at both ends and rather long, they are liable to be dangerous, so bear in mind the safety points already outlined. Remember they concern:

(a) return throwing;
(b) method of carrying;
(c) where to put javelins not in use;
(d) how to collect and return javelins;
(e) care to be exercised when pulling javelins out of the ground;
(f) the distance between throwers at practice;
(g) when to throw;
(h) where to throw.

As with discus throwing and shot putting, you can get in most practice when you are working alone or in a very small group and you have a number of implements, or one implement and a throwing net.

LEARNING TO THROW (right-handed)
Things to Do

(a) Take a javelin and place it in your right hand, which you are
holding palm uppermost. I suggest the claw or two finger grip,
as in photograph 39. The javelin slots between the first and
second fingers which can now press or pull on the back of the
binding. The javelin will lie along the palm of the hand and along
the forearm.

39. Get a grip. These boys show three ways of holding the javelin so that you can pull
on the binding. One of the commonest ways, in the centre, is the claw grip. Some
throwers believe that the grip demonstrated on the right helps to make the javelin land
point first because the first finger is stretched back underneath.

(b) Now try running along holding the javelin high overhead, not
close to your shoulder. The palm of the hand will face upwards,
the 'heel' of the hand will face the front.

(c) Throw the javelin from the overhead position with the left foot
forward. Throw it into the ground two or three yards in front of
you.

40. Running along holding the javelin whilst the coach helps with the fundamentals of the carry. It's an enjoyable preliminary practice and safe when lines of the track are used as guides.

41. Here we see boys and girls doing target javelin throwing with close proximity targets.

(d) Walk along with the javelin held overhead and then when you have taken a few walking strides and as the left foot is coming to the ground, throw the javelin into the ground as in (c).

(e) Improve on (d) by turning the body slightly and taking the arm a little further back before throwing. The hips are still facing forward.

(f) Remember that you are throwing, not bowling a cricket ball, so the elbow of the throwing arm comes through and is rapidly straightened even though the javelin comes from an overhead position. After jogging a few strides—six will do—gather yourself and throw as before, making the javelin stick in. Keep the hips facing forward.

(g) Jog with the javelin overhead and as you approach the last five or six strides and you feel you must gather to throw, start to turn the shoulders and take the javelin back with an athletically bent arm, keeping the hips more or less to the front. As your feet now come to the ground further and further in front, the body will be leaning back so the throw can be made off the last long stride with a pull and throw. Use targets and gradually increase the range.

(h) You can now begin to think of throwing on the run which is really an improvement of practice (g). The important strides are the last six. When you get to these, turn your shoulders and take the javelin back, stretching the arm and keeping the palm up but the head and hips to the front. As the right foot comes through on stride five, you should be leaning back. As you land from a gather and move over the right foot you must reach out a little more than normal with the left foot so that you throw off your right and over the left. As in shot and discus, keep your left shoulder up by lifting the left arm. Keep it up until the javelin has left.

It is important that both the performer and the helper bear in mind the principles or fundamental thinking which should be going on whilst the practices take place. Here are just a few of the more important points:

(i) Whilst about a dozen strides might be sufficient for you at first, you can eventually run about thirteen to sixteen strides—more for adults.

(ii) Have a short approach—six or seven strides at first. These include gathering and throwing strides.

(iii) You should be throwing on the run—not run, stop, throw.

(iv) Speed and power come only after much practice, so control your efforts.

(v) Too many full-out throws without a proper warm-up and with bad technique will give you a sore elbow.

(vi) If, when you throw, you cannot feel the weight of the javelin and you have nothing to pull and throw, then your arm has come through too quickly.

(vii) Practice means doing hundreds of throws, but by no means all are full-out efforts.

(viii) Do not worry about scratch lines or throwing lines. You can adjust your run to fit in with the official markings later.

(ix) Estimate your run up, throw and stopping distance by doing the activity freely, measuring what distance you need and putting that behind the throwing arc.

(x) The different ways of gripping the javelin are shown in photograph 39. Try all these methods, adopting the one you like best and which produces the best results. A 'V' grip often helps prevent a sore elbow.

(xi) What you are trying to do is to get as much of your arm moving as fast as possible with as much weight behind it as possible at the moment of release. The shoulders lead the arm. The method used here, with hips to the front, was used initially by the Finns. It is really the least complicated method of achieving this.

(xii) If the javelin is not landing point first, then as you throw ensure that the point is lower at release than it was in the previous attempt.

(xiii) Keep the javelin pointing forward as you run and throw and you will have more chance of throwing it straight. Correct hand alignment—make sure you rotate your wrist to force the palm upward.

(xiv) Only run at a speed you can control, thus running smoothly into your throw. Thirteen to fifteen strides should be ample.

(xv) As the javelin is taken back prior to throwing, rotate your forearm to make the palm really face upwards.

RULES

The rules are given in the AAA Handbook, but here are a few important points from them.

The javelin is thrown from behind an arc of 28 degrees and an area marked as in the diagram. The throw is measured from the inside of the arc to the mark made by the point of the javelin, provided it lands within the sector. To get a correct measurement, the tape is run out from the point X as shown by the dotted line and the distance measured Y to Z. The athlete must throw from behind the arc and not go on to or over line and arc A-B.

42. Novice javelin throwers run to a line, in this case the edge of a track, before throwing. The white marker designates a throwing place.

43 and 44. *(above left and above)*
Early attempts may not match the
technique and style of champions but
trying is important. Full marks to this
schoolboy for effort. Look how he has
tried to throw right 'through' the javelin
also turning his shoulder before using
the arm.

45. *(left)* This is the way to get into a
throwing position from the run up. This
action picture of Pru Fiend at Crystal
Palace shows how to continue running
with the hips fairly well turned to the
front whilst the arms and shoulder are
sideways to the throw.

46. *(above)* How to get a long last stride is well illustrated in this competition throw by Shara Spragg of Cheltenham. With the left heel about to come down well to the front, she will have a good base to throw from.

47. *(right)* Sharon Corbett threw 48 metres in the Midlands Womens Championship. The features to note here are the well-arched back, the hips leading, left leg well in front and knee bent ready to drive as the body moves forward and over it.

Summary of points for you and your coach to watch at the throw.

1. Try to see that the javelin is thrown from overhead, not past the ear.
2. The shoulders are brought round to the front first, the arms whip through last. Use your body.
3. The last stride is a long one and left foot comes down slightly to the left of the line of throw.
4. When the javelin is taken back, the hips should not be turned sideways with the body. The degree of body mobility is a determining factor here.
5. The drive for the throw begins on the right foot.
6. The front leg (left) which checks the forward speed is bent, making a long last stride (Olympic throwers stride about 3·3 metres).
7. The right foot comes to the ground heel first, facing or almost facing the front, thus tending to help in the effort to keep the hips to the front. Note that the right hip will drive in as the left foot comes down on the last stride.

48. This schoolgirl at the ESAA Championships, competing in the Intermediate Group, shows a high delivery with a relaxed but speedy arm coming through whilst still in contact with the ground.

8. Since the legs and shoulder are in position before the arm pull, there tends to be an arched back at the start of the throwing action (see photograph 47). The hip will have been driven in ahead of the shoulders.

9. In order to keep your throwing palm in the right position, keep the forearm rotated outwards as you take the javelin back.

10. During the throw, as the shoulders come round, the left arm is flung round at shoulder level with the elbow leading. As the right elbow starts to lead the throwing movement it may be higher than the palm of the hand. Do not anticipate the throw by bending the arm too soon.

11. The left arm, shoulder and leg form the firm side and base from which the throw is made.

12. The finger can impart rotation to the javelin so that it 'rifles' through the air.

13. The thrower may appear to step or run away slightly to the side as the long last stride is taken, thus allowing the javelin to be kept in line with the direction of throw.

49. Brian Roberts of St Pauls College, Cheltenham competing in the inter-counties championship and throwing 78·38 metres. Check the 'points' of technique from the text.

14. The forward momentum after throwing is stopped by doing a reverse. This may mean a number of hops on the right leg and space to do it in, possibly after a jump leg change.

Once you can throw the spear, like all athletes, you improve by getting stronger, faster and technically more competent. So throw often but in a free and easy sort of way, thus avoiding tennis elbow and back strain.

Aim to do a set number of 'relaxed' throws and a much fewer number of competition-type throws. Start with a total of, say, fifty a week, rising to over a hundred later.

Practise particular parts of the technique by doing the whole throw but paying special attention to the part of the movement you or the observer thinks requires it. Have an observer even if you cannot get a coach.

Basically, you are trying to achieve (i) acceleration into the throw and (ii) arm speed.

Use a net with a specially adapted javelin to get lots of throws without having to get the javelin.

50. L. Osborne of Sussex at the ESAA Championships, 'lifts' the javelin away. Note she is still in contact with the ground and has used her legs and a fast arm to throw right through the spear.

WHAT IS A GOOD THROW?

Here are some sample standards and grades from the ESAA Minimum School Standards required for National Entry for Javelin.

Javelin

		Boys	*Girls*
Junior		(600 gms) 41·60 metres	(600 gms) 28·04 metres
Intermediate		(700 gms) 50·50 metres	(600 gms) 32·24 metres
Senior		(800 gms) 53·90 metres	(600 gms) 34·24 metres

At a schools meeting the standards expected would be as follows:

		Boys	*Girls*
Junior	Under 13	24·00 metres	16·20 metres
	Under 14	29·20 metres	19·60 metres
	Under 15	32·40 metres	22·00 metres
Intermediate	Under 16	38·40 metres	23·50 metres
	Under 17	41·40 metres	24·80 metres
Senior	Under 18	45·10 metres	25·80 metres
	Under 19	46·30 metres	26·70 metres
	Under 20	47·00 metres	27·30 metres

See also Five Star Award Charts.

5. THROWING THE HAMMER

The hammer used in athletic competition does not really look like a hammer at all. For men's events it is a 7·25 kg weight on the end of 120 cm of wire; for Junior boys a 4 kg ball on 120 cm of wire. There is a handle for gripping so that it can be swung round and round before letting it fly off.

Like all the other throwing implements it can be a dangerous weapon when carelessly used and if it is not cared for when not in use. When the hammer lands it impacts the ground and knocks up divots, and these two factors mean that there is always difficulty in finding somewhere both safe and acceptable for practice and competition.

Practice hammers, where sandbags or chains have been substituted for the iron ball, are in common use as they help to prevent damage to landing surfaces. Safety nets, the use of out-of-the-way areas and limiting of access to these places help towards greater safety. Individuals wishing to practise have sought out quarries, disused corners of airfields and waste tips, as well as having special times when they can throw more or less alone on games and sports areas.

Particular care must be taken of the implement itself for one peculiar hazard is the breaking of the wire during a swing. It rarely happens and should not happen at all, but the warning must be given. If you are watching a hammer being thrown, stand well back and on the side where the swinging hammer is coming down low. If anything breaks at that point, then at least the hammer will go into the ground first before travelling on in that direction.

You should ensure that the hammer itself is safe by checking that

(a) the wire is not frayed;

(b) the head swivels easily and the nuts and rivets are safe;

(c) the wire is not kinked;

(d) any twists in the wire are not unwinding;

(e) there has been no rusting;

(f) at the end of a session the implement is hung vertically and not left lying about;

(g) before each throw you check swivels and wire.

If normal safety precautions are adopted, this is as safe as any throwing event and perhaps safer than many situations on the games field.

SOME FUNDAMENTALS

As with all throwing events, you are endeavouring to build up speed in the implement and then release it at the correct angle.

The main force will come from accelerating turns which you make by swinging the hammer round your head first, and then by turning yourself to fit in with the circling implement.

The arc through which the hammer is swung has a low point in front of the right foot and a high point in the direction of the left shoulder for a right-hander swinging anti-clockwise.

The release is over the left shoulder.

The hammer can only be swung as fast as you have weight and strength to counterbalance its desire to go off in a straight line.

Counterbalancing is best done if a semi-squat position is adopted.

When you turn you should try to get the maximum speed at the end and stretch the legs to get lift at release, keeping a firm base.

The turning movement with the hammer is not a smooth, even one. Hips and body lead, then there is a slight pause whilst the hammer catches up, and then the hips, body and shoulders lead round again quickly. The hammer accelerates, nearly catches up and after one or more turns, is thrown from a firm standing base. Greater velocity is achieved by doing more than one turn.

51. *(above)* Ian Chipchase has speed, weight, and skill to counterbalance this swinging ball. Notice his straight arms and feet on the ground as he is about to release this senior boys hammer.

51 and 53. *(above right and right)* A selection of hammers, including the sandbag variety, of different lengths. The ball on the grass has a handle directly attached to the ball.

LEARNING TO THROW (right-handed thrower)
Standing Throw

First select a hammer you can handle. Make a sandbag hammer or have a short wire put on a normal light hammer. It is essential here to be able to cope with the forces or pulls that your swinging hammer sets up. Get a good grip. If you are right-handed you need to grip with your left hand first. Some throwers wear a glove on the hand in contact with the metal.

1. Stand with your back to the direction in which you wish to throw and swing the implement round the head without moving from the feet-short-astride position. When throwing over the left shoulder,

55

54. Swinging practice with sandbag hammer. Lot of space required here.

55. Missiles gone. First attempts with the implement going over the left shoulder.

swing anti-clockwise, with the right hand over the left. Do lots of this swinging with shortened wire or rope. You could even have the handle attached directly to the ball for a start but make sure it is securely done. No release.

2. Next, do similar movements getting a low and high point in the swing. Put a mark opposite the right foot—this is where the low point will be. No release.

3. If you have had a shortened 'wire' then extend it so that you can cope with the wider swinging arc. More free swings.

4. Swing the hammer round until you feel that you are controlling it and that your feet are not being lifted off the ground. Try to keep the knees bent. Try accelerating and decelerating. Do not worry about minor points of technique. Swing the hammer emphasizing the lifting part of the swing. Still no turning of the body. As in 3. but let the hammer go over the left shoulder. At the high point the arms and hands will stretch out over the shoulder. Throw on, say, the third swing, stretching the legs as the move is performed. Reach out after the hammer. Have some competition throwing over the shoulder, standing throws with limited circling. Remember to use your legs and arms in the final lift as the hammer flies off over the left shoulder.

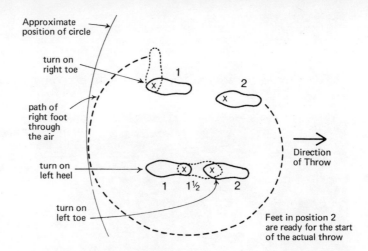

Approximate
position of circle

turn on
right toe

path of
right foot
through
the air

Diagram F. Foot
movements in a single
turn.

turn on
left heel

turn on
left toe

Direction
of Throw

Feet in position 2
are ready for the start
of the actual throw

THE TURN

It is a good idea, if you get the chance, to look at a performer or an action
film and then try the following. Assuming you have not done this turning
before, try out these activities.

1. Without bothering about the preliminary swings, just shuffle round
   as the hammer swings. As you move round holding the hammer,
   you will feel it pulling. Watch the ball and keep the arms straight
   and the knees bent. Do not release the hammer. Do a number of
   turns like this so that you get used to controlling the pull as you go
   round. Try not to bend the arms.
2. Now turn as in 1. but by moving the arms up and down, get the
   low point in front and the high point over the shoulder. Do not
   release the hammer yet but do try to get a rhythm in the swings. It
   will not be a fast swing at this stage.
3. Next, after two or three swings round the head, go into your
   shuffling turn. Do not release the hammer.
4. After two or three preliminary swings go into a shuffle turn and
   release over the left shoulder.

At this stage, you should not worry about the foot movements; just
turn using a shuffle or even a discus-type turn. The important thing is to
get round before the hammer and have your back to the direction of
throw early ready to release over the left shoulder. The aim is to be in
control of the hammer.

You should by now at least be able to do some sort of turn and release.

56. Quite good for a beginner's first effort. There are not many who do better than this at the start.

The Heel Toe Turn (anti-clockwise)

Once you begin to feel more secure and able to cope as you turn round, you should start on the proper foot movements.

1. Stand with your back to the direction of throw and astride the direction-of-throw line.
2. Let your body weight go over the left heel and as you do so, start to turn.
3. Turn on the heel quickly and as you turn your hips, shoulders and head through 360 degrees, you will have to transfer your weight along the outside of your left foot to the toe. It is a heel, outer border of foot, base of toes action. Note, this is done without the hammer at first. Turn on the left heel leaving the right foot in contact with the ground. Bent knees are essential when doing turns, particularly the left knee.

57. *(above)* A shot of the feet as the boys, who are learning the hammer, practise.

58. *(right)* Coming along nicely. A release after doing a turn.

4. As in 3. but emphasizing the spin on the left toe and the rapid pick up and move round of the right leg as it hastens to get into position, having been 'left behind' as the heel turn was made.

5. Try the turn with a hammer with a shortened wire.

6. At some point, try two turns without the hammer and then try turning with a hammer you can handle.

7. Try single or double turns establishing a rhythm which emphasizes the down and up of the swings.

You will be finding that the combining of the swings and turns presents a problem. A basic technique will evolve as you try out combinations of the points and activities mentioned, i.e. emphasizing a rhythm or count, practising with and without a hammer, shortening the wire, fastening the handle directly to the shot, doing one turn only, turning without an implement, and increasing and decreasing the velocity of the swings.

You can practise turns indoors, without a hammer (or with a hammer

if you protect the floor. A sandbag hammer is usually used indoors).
Think of the two parts: (a) left heel; (b) left toe and right leg coming
round quickly but near the floor.

59. This is how the thrower starts. Notice the glove worn on the left hand for protection. As from 1973 the glove must be a mitten and allow the ends of the fingers to be seen.

60. Howard Payne leaves the hammer behind as he goes into his turns. Always in contact with the ground, he gets his right leg round quickly and his hips and shoulders. Note the straight left arm.

IMPROVING PERFORMANCE

Try to:

   (a) Keep the hammer head as far away as possible in large swings.

   (b) Bend the arms only as they come overhead in preliminary swings.

   (c) Keep the arms straight in the turn. They should be straight and act merely as an extension to the wire. They are straight even in the final fling.

61. Here the strong Barry Williams is able to turn and keep his arms straight. You can see how he is pivoting on the outer border of his foot as he moves and turns into this throw. No leaning back with straight legs like the learners, and look at the bent knee.

(d) Keep your back straight.

(e) Lean away from the hammer with bent knees.

(f) Keep in front of the hammer as you turn. Lead it round.

(g) Look out and not at the feet. Keep your head up.

(h) Get half your turn on the ball of the foot and keep balance.

(i) Avoid a jump as you turn. Slow down if you are being lifted.

(j) Make the feet and hips lead the movement.

(k) Do two turns fairly competently before going on to three.

(l) Ensure contact with the ground all the time. Without this there can be no acceleration.

(m) Drive upwards and outwards with arms and legs on the delivery.

(n) Move along a straight delivery line as you turn.

(o) As you make the slight pause between turns make sure your knees are bent, with the weight on the left leg and the right foot just touching the ground each time.

62 and 63. *(above)* Compare these two pictures. One shows the sort of thing you will do during your first attempts, the other Howard Payne a competitor in the 1964, 68 and 72 Olympics. Note Paynes 'sitting' position, straight arms and feet on the ground, ready to drive into the final turn. Payne has control and balance. The schoolboy will need more practice with lighter hammers on shorter wires.

64. *(left)* This photograph shows the effort put into the throw by Stan Douglas in the Intermediate Group at the ESAA Championships, the judge outside the net looks for faults.

(p) Lead off quickly into each turn.

(q) Push the elbows together.

(r) Your maximum speed should be at the end of the turns.

(s) Stay in the circle by lowering your body weight.

(t) Keep the arms more or less passive as the legs drive up for the release.

(u) Increase hammer speed by the hip and body turns, not by the arms pulling round.

(v) Emphasize the bent left leg in anti-clockwise turns.

TRAINING

Skill at the movement will only come from practice so spend a lot of time doing the whole of the movement rather than parts of it. Practise with different weights and lengths of wire. Nylon cord is easier to handle than wire and is often used in practices. A carefully and safely constructed home-made chain hammer is a useful implement. Use a 5-inch steel key ring and slide on lengths of chain each about a foot long. Weight can thus be adjusted at will. A handle can be attached, using a nylon cord.

Nylon cord threaded through a short piece of garden hose and bent into a triangular hammer handle makes a useful practice handle for attaching to a sandbag or chains.

If you are taking up the event seriously, you need to develop strength and to put on some weight. So, although practising throwing will develop muscle power, it is not enough in itself. Here weight training is a must.

Speed and general fitness are required and here running of various types will help. Try out other events, particularly throws and jumps.

Training sessions should be done every day but need only be short, perhaps forty minutes to one hour. Divide the time between techniques, general fitness and strength and speed work.

An hour's session might be divided up as follows:

A.

1. Warm-up—jogging and some preliminary hammer swinging—5 minutes.

2. Practise throwing with turns in groups of four throws. Measure the best of each four—say five lots of four—40 minutes.
3. Sprinting—4×50 metres.

B.
1. Warm-up using preliminary swings and free standing exercises.
2. Technique practices—practise turning with hammers of various sizes. Work inside a circle. Start with standing throws to get a feel, then move on to full turns.
3. Weight Training. Strengthening work for the legs in particular, but all round strength is required and body bulk is also an asset in this event.

Note that technique and strength and weight development should take place side by side. The two are inter-related.

A FEW STATISTICS

Qualifying standards for 1972 Nationals.

Boys Hammer

Junior	4 kg	34·56 metres
Intermediate	5 kg	38·50 metres
Senior	6·25 kg	42·50 metres

Standard Attainment ESAA Grades.

Boys Hammer

		I	II	III	IV
U.15 Junior	4 kgs	32·12	30·18	27·78	25·30 metres
U.17 Intermediate	5 kgs	34·00	31·50	29·00	26·00 metres
U.18 Senior	6·25 kgs	32·00	29·00	26·00	25·00 metres
U.20 Senior	6·25 kgs	40·00	37·00	34·50	32·00 metres

See also Five Star Award Charts

An Interesting Rule

The general rules for throwing apply but remember that, although you are allowed to stop and start again, the hammer head must not touch the circle once you have started the turn.

5. CROSS COUNTRY RUNNING

GENERAL BACKGROUND

Many of the most famous athletic clubs in the country have the word Harriers included in their name. There is a long tradition in this aspect of athletics and running over the country has taken, and still takes, many forms. Fell running, round the houses races, road races, road relays, marathons, hare and hounds, and 'paper' chases are some of the variations on cross country running. Cross country, as we now know it, is a circuit of a course of anything up to about 7 miles set out over the local terrain and perhaps including plough, grass, woodland, steep and gentle slope, stiles, fences, and road.

More recently in this country orienteering has become a recognized sport. This is competitive and involves finding a way over varied terrain by map and compass.

Because of international competition the tendency today is to go for cross country courses which are fairly flat over even country where the runners can be seen, but there are many who prefer more varied and interesting courses.

In the British Isles, with its particular weather, cross country has never been a summer sport. It takes place from Autumn through Winter and into Spring. A cross country match is rarely cancelled or postponed because of weather, so those who take it up at club level are sure of regular participation. In schools, the run is a regular substitute for a washed out games period and an addition to normal cross country work.

65

65 and 66. They're off. Soon after the start it's really bumpy going and not only underfoot—the competitors must jockey for space. They don't want to be queueing at the first gap in the hedge or along the next narrow path.

STARTING CROSS COUNTRY RUNNING

Many have started cross country running because they first used it as a training for some other sport or game, others have come to it because they found it a non-personal contact sport, simple in organization, needing very little equipment and an event which could be practised at any time with or without companions.

If you are a beginner it is important that you enjoy your running and leave intense competitive racing until you have logged up a good mileage of running over the country and had lots of time trials.

First, choose a circuit of road or country and jog over the distance. You may even use a mixture of jogging, running and walking in the first instance. At the age of about 11 or 12, $\frac{3}{4}$–1 mile can be far enough.

Next, start to time yourself over your chosen course and keep a record of your times. You will find some quite big improvements over the first few weeks, though you must be prepared for the odd drop in time now and then and also for your times to stay fairly level at certain stages. Do this in reverse by seeing how much ground you can cover in a set time, say 15 minutes.

67. Parkland courses are popular and certainly make good training country.

It is also useful to work in a group, running and jogging across the countryside. Here you should vary the distance and type of terrain if possible so that you each begin to discover your strengths and weaknesses, likes and dislikes; for example, who runs best uphill, who is best over fields, and so on.

Once you feel that cross country is going to be a major sport for you, you might do more specialist training and plan ahead.

TRAINING FOR OLDER BOYS AND GIRLS

Once your Summer activities such as track athletics, are over, your training for cross country starts. Cross country racing is a team event as well as an individual one so, rather like relay racing, there is a need for team practices as well as individual training sessions.

Aims: You are aiming chiefly for improvement in your stamina, your skill and tactical knowledge, all of which help to improve your time over the distance.

67

Your stamina can be built up by:

(a) uphill walks and long walks at a good pace;

(b) races uphill;

(c) running in boots or with a weighted belt;

(d) running over difficult terrain, e.g. soft earth, sand, etc.;

(e) Fartlek training.

The distance you choose should be related to the time you take, the distance you are training for and the type of country, but the work should be a challenge. (See the chapter on Middle Distance Running in *Better Athletics—Track*.)

68. Soon after the start of this school cross country race there was a rush for the gate. Note the natural low carriage of the majority of runners. The leader seems to be aware of the mass of runners and is sprinting for the exit.

YOUR SKILL AND RACE TACTICS

Here are some points which you should bear in mind when racing:

1. Keep in contact with the leaders, or at least with a group of about your ability.

2. Make sure you know the course so that you know where passing is possible, where the hills are and what kind of surface you will have to run on.

3. Judge your pace by other runners you know and are in contact with, by the terrain, and by your own feelings. Pace judgement is the basis of all types of long distance running.

4. At the start of a race there are often masses of runners who sprint off at a fast pace. Keep in touch but do not follow too closely. Pace yourself and you will be with the others as they drop into their more realistic slower speed.

5. Encourage and help each other by running as a group. Some will be better running uphill, some better over rough ground, and so on.

6. As a front runner you should try to break contact, so develop the ability to go hard at particular times. Freedom from having to repeat level laps on a track will provide you with varied opportunities for increasing a lead or catching up.

7. Just as you can increase a lead so others can come up on you if you are not constantly on the alert. Do not drop into a monotonous, unthinking plod. Changing pace and running pattern for a few strides helps to fight off the feeling of tiredness.

8. When running on flat ground you should use an efficient running form which usually means a low arm carriage, and much less knee lift and drive than the middle distance runner would use.

9. Over rough ground rhythm is maintained by adopting a shorter stride and using the arms for balance. You will have to watch the surface carefully, often picking places for your feet.

10. When running uphill, shorten your stride but keep the rhythm. Leaning forward helps.

11. When running downhill, lengthen your stride. If you can get away whilst others are doing an enforced slower uphill run, then this is to your advantage. Keep the body upright and control your speed.

12. Negotiating obstacles on a course presents problems. Ankle and leg damage is prevented and speed maintained by:
    (a) hopping rather than leaping when coming off embankments;
    (b) running through ditches and streams instead of doing jarring jumps over them;
    (c) landing on two feet if the landing side of a fence is uneven, though a side vault is often quicker if you can do it safely and well.

13. When you pass someone in a race on the track or over the country, do so in a determined way so that you open a gap. This applies to you individually and to the members of the team you are running with.

14. When running as a group you should let the lead change and sometimes even allow an opponent to lead, thus taking the head winds. Run just behind him but do not watch his feet.

15. Try to get in front before reaching parts of the course where passing is difficult, such as narrow trails and stiles.

16. Cross country is a team event, therefore all the members of the team count. A single place gained by, say, someone in the 80s can influence a team's position.

69. Uphill running means shorter strides. Those who got to the top first can break away.

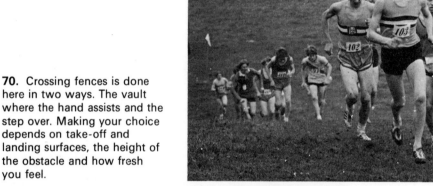

70. Crossing fences is done here in two ways. The vault where the hand assists and the step over. Making your choice depends on take-off and landing surfaces, the height of the obstacle and how fresh you feel.

71. Here you see where a fence has been removed for safety. This youngster seems to have reached the gap before the crowd of runners. Note the marker flag.

72. A pleasant run through the country as well as the pressure of competition. On this narrow path she will be difficult to pass. Yes, gloves and long sleeves for cold days.

73. A typical ditch and bog makes life difficult but interesting. See how a queue forms as competitors hesitate and pick their way. All to the advantage of No 10.

74. A sprint to the finish in a minors competition.

CROSS COUNTRY EQUIPMENT

Just as the track and field event athletes have different types of shoes for different events, so cross country runners must change footwear for different courses.

If you are running on an all-grass course, you can use short spikes set fairly wide to prevent turning the ankle. Also use small spikes for icy surfaces. Where terrain is mixed and you have to run on a road, a leather shoe with rubber studs is most suitable.

Heel pads are a must and light woollen socks help to prevent chafed toes. Well-fitted shoes are important.

In Winter you can choose between long-sleeved vests, lightweight jerseys, and games shirts that are loose under the armpits. They have all proved more satisfactory than the thin singlet so useful in warmer weather. Gloves are a must for cold weather and grease can be used on the body as a heat retainer.

75. *(left)* Unless you have firmly fitting shoes you would be in trouble in this morass on the Midlands Cross Country Course. See the rather wide arms for balance. Eyes show that he is really picking his way through.

76. *(right)* Across the fields and through the stream. It is often better to step through shallow streams rather than leap through them. Leaping breaks the rhythm and jars the body, but if the stream bed is an unknown quantity, you must leap.

LOOK AFTER YOURSELF

1. General health and fitness are important so don't miss any training.
2. Warm up before running.
3. Don't stand around getting cold after racing or training.
4. Find out what foods suit you on the day of a race or when hard training is imminent. Usually fatty, greasy foods are unsuitable. Some runners go for as long as four hours without solid food before racing, though they take drinks and sugars.
5. Try to arrive at a competition in good time so that you have a chance to view the course.
6. Always complete the course, both in practice and on the day. This will help you to prove your determination and develop endurance.
7. Distance running takes quite a lot out of you. You need sleep to put it back, so make sure you get plenty.

77. *(left)* Into a finishing funnel. This young runner is receiving a disc with his position number on it. He will give it to his team manager.

78. *(right)* They all finished in a bunch but in the narrow funnel they are forced to keep their finishing order. Note the shirts under the vests on this cold day.

73

RULES—A FEW IMPORTANT POINTS

Scoring. 'At the conclusion of a race, the places of all the competitors having been decided, the judges and officials shall add together the respective places of the scoring competitors of each team, and the team with the lowest aggregate will be declared the winner.

'In the event of a team tie the team whose last scoring member finishes nearer the first place shall be the winners.'—rule.

Courses must be clearly marked.

The numbers allowed to run for each team and how many are to count must be declared beforehand. In the ESAA it is six to run from each county, with four to count.

It is difficult to have universal standards of an attainment in an event where courses vary from place to place and which also change with the weather. Usually the sort of records which are kept are those of best performance for a particular course for a particular age group and sex.

At school level, courses are as short as 1 mile, though for boys the Junior (under 15) distances may go up to but not be more than 5,000 metres, the Intermediates (under 17) up to 6,500 metres, whilst the Seniors are limited to 8,000 metres.

The maximum girls distances are: under 15—2,500 metres; under 17—3,250 metres; under 20—4,000 metres.

7. RACE WALKING

Although walking is something we all do every day, too few people think of trying it competitively. Even if you have not succeeded at the technical events and games of skill, if you enjoy walking and are prepared to practise technique, race walking might be just the event for you to take up.

GENERAL POINTS

There are championships at various levels in this event and they are held on the track and on the roads. The Race Walking Association arranges these, often in conjunction with the AAA, and there are competitions at school level.

Junior competitions take place over distances of from 1–5 miles, or or 1,500 metres to 8,000 metres, on track or road.

The seniors walk up to 50 kilometres in competition.

LEADING UP TO RACE WALKING

1. You must practise by taking part in kiking and generally covering both short and long distances at fast walking speeds.
2. Start to time yourself over distances, as well as measuring distances you can cover in particular times.
3. Have a few short walking races—say, over 100 or 400 metres.

Important Note

Make sure you really walk all the time. No cheating. According to the Race Walking Association, walking is 'making progress by steps so that unbroken contact with the ground is maintained'. You must put the front foot down before the rear foot comes off the ground.

LEARNING THE TECHNIQUE OF RACE WALKING

1. Try leaning the body in different positions when you walk—forward, backward or upright. You will probably discover that when you lean forward you cannot put your feet down quite so far in front of you so you have to keep your body fairly upright in order to take a longer stride. A fairly upright carriage is important.

2. Try to concentrate on keeping your head and body more or less upright and carried on the hips in a steady position.

79. A schools walking race. All sizes, all trying, keenness but no tension. Notice the characteristic arm swing across the body. This photograph taken just after the start of the Midlands Junior Championship shows the jockeying at the start and how a turn of speed can get competitors out of the ruck.

3. Now try to increase the stride by using the hips (see diagram). You will see how you can increase stride length and walk on a line by correct use of the hips. You should deliberately push the hip forward on the leading side and then as the drive is finished, bring the other side through low. The hip is lowest when that leg is

moving forward. The other hip, moving back, will be correspond-
ingly higher. The stride is thus made along and close to the ground,
the bending of the knee allowing the leg to come through without
trailing the ground (see photograph). The hip movement is quite
a feature of race walking as the athlete tries to reach forward making
use of the hips and yet lift the hip to allow the recovery of the

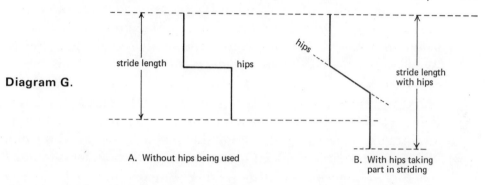

Diagram G.

stride length   hips   hips   stride length with hips

A. Without hips being used   B. With hips taking part in striding

80. *(left)* The good form of No 3 is taking him into the lead at this point in the Midlands Junior Championship. Can you see the tensions of No 34 and his loss of form as he struggles to keep the lead? See also the good leg drive, level shoulders and upright carriage of No 3.
81. *(right)* Continuing good form of No 3 as he strides ahead with a good lead.

trailing leg as it swings forward. This leads to a rolling gait—a 'sinking' on the one side and a lift on the other—with the shoulders held level. The hip which is on the supporting side is high. This up and down backward circling of the hips allows the walker to travel smoothly without bobbing up and down.

4. Walk short distances, concentrating on the driving and swing through of the legs. The action is a heel-toe one. As the hip comes round the leg is thrust forward, coming to the ground fractionally before the other leg has finished its drive, with a good ankle stretch. As the rest of the leading foot comes to the ground the body moves over and the hip swings round ready to be driven forward again.

5. Stand with feet astride and with the arms bent at the elbows, fists lightly clenched. Swing the arms from the shoulders alternately to a centre line in front of the chest and to a point just behind the hip. This swinging of the arms without shrugging the shoulders simulates the correct movement when walking. Practise this in front of a mirror.

6. Now set off walking deliberately, speeding up and slowing down the arm movements. Note how they affect the legs. Try not to lift, shrug or tense the shoulders.

7. Walk at a moderate non-race pace, gradually increasing effort but concentrating on bringing the recovery foot through close to the ground and quickly. You might find it helpful to turn the foot out slightly as it passes the supporting foot. Gradually increase the length of time you walk at full pace using the heel-toe movement and low rapid carry-through action.

8. Once you have got a basic technique of walking, work on improving your technique and building up your endurance. If you make yourself more supple and mobile about the hips, you can increase your stride length.

Here are some points for your friend or coach to look for when you practise technique. These apply to road race walking or track race walking.

82. *(above)* No 23 might be overdoing the across body arm swing a feature of all the walkers. Look at No 4 and notice how his left foot is coming through near the track whilst the supporting right hip is high. By swinging his left hip forward he is lengthening his stride.

83. *(above right)* What a good idea. A mixed race with E. Smith of Warley catching the boys in the competition for intermediates.

84. *(right)* P. Bransom winning the 2500 metres walk for Juniors. She is really losing style by dropping hips and shoulders in the effort to lengthen her stride without 'lifting'.

1. The head and shoulders should be level and not move up and down as you walk.
2. The leg should be thrust out in front to let the heel come down as far forward as possible. In order to achieve this, full ankle stretch is necessary.
3. There must be a full drive from the leg concerned, with hip, knee and ankle fully extended. No 'bent knee creeps' due to rigid ankles.
4. The knee of the leg being recovered should come through without too much bend. High knee lift wastes energy and time.
5. Lack of split at the thighs, giving short strides and an appearance of squatting when walking, could either mean lack of mobility or that you are forgetting to stretch at the hips and knees.
6. The shoulders are sometimes tensed and shrugged in an effort to lift the body. Try to relax the arms so that movements are controlled but not tense.
7. There should be no 'lifting'. This is not uncommon when competition is keen and the walking has really become bounding.
8. Make sure the rhythm is even and smooth without any stops.
9. The body should be held erect. Do not imitate those head-on-one-side, one-sided walkers. You should get even drive and support and recovery movements.

TRAINING

Whilst you are improving your technique, your endurance and speed will be built up by weight training and exercises for mobility. Try a few of the following:
1. Go for long walks through the countryside. Stroll part of the way and walk quickly over other stretches. Keep a log of time taken and distance covered. Your distance will be related to your competition distance, as will the amount of fast walking included. A mile in 12 or 13 minutes is a reasonably fast general walking pace. You might try walking a little faster over a shorter distance, doing a mile

85. *(left)* Good striding with extended legs and shoulders square and level. The heel is down just as the rear toes leave, giving a good split at the thighs, and Paul Nihil Champion Walker reaches the line first to win again.

86. *(right)* You can see here how a slight bend of the right knee enables the right foot to come through near the ground. Lack of tension should be noted.

in slightly less time—say, 10 minutes which is really quite a fast non-race walk for you as a beginner.

2. Accelerate your speed and then wind down to an amble, concentrating on points of technique.

3. Interval sprint walking. Bursts of 50 metres flat out followed by a recovery period of 50 metres strolling.

4. Hill walking—some sprinting down slopes.

5. Timed walks. Try to walk as far as you can in a set time. If the time is a short one—say, 2 minutes—then these can be repeated.

6. (a) Hurdling exercises for mobility.

   (b) The stairs exercise. Toes on the stair edge, ankles bending and stretching. Your heels will thus be able to go below the level of the toes and so add range to the movement in the ankles which is not possible when standing on the floor.

(c) Walking down an inclined plank with feet flat—mainly for ankle extension. The slope can be increased as ankle extension improves.

(d) Down-hill running accelerating and decelerating.

If you are just starting competitive walking, the 1-mile track event or the 3-mile road race walk are the ones to choose. As you get stronger, increased distances can be attempted.

Race walking shoes are built to give protection, particularly to the heels, and they are strong and light. Prevention of blisters is important and those of you who have done cross country or hill walking, or played football on a bone-hard pitch, know how quickly blisters come and how incapacitating they can be.

Use good, well-fitting walking shoes, wash your feet and wear woollen socks with heel pads. A liberal application of soft soap on the socks before a competition will help to prevent rubbing.

If you go out on the roads, wear a distinctive colour and fluorescent bib of the type used by road workers and the police. Use the pavements when possible and, of course, do your road work at quiet traffic times.

In the ESAA there is as yet no walking competition for girls, but for boys there are competitions at Junior, Intermediate and Senior Level.

To give you some idea of times and distances the best performances, as at May 1972, are:

	Junior	Inter	Senior
3,000 metres	14m.8s.	12m.56·6s.	—
5,000 metres	—	—	23m.13·4s.

There are standards set by the ESAA for this event and they are:

	Grade I	Grade II	Grade III	Grade IV
3,000 metres Inter U.17	16·00	17·00	18·00	19·00
3,000 metres Inter U.16	16·15	17·15	18·15	19·25
3,000 metres Jun. U.15	16·40	17·35	18·45	20·00
5,000 metres Sen. U.17	27·45	29·30	31·00	33·00

82

87 and 88. We all have to start somewhere. The walkers featured in 87 are probably getting as much excitement from their event as the walker showing good form and competing in the stadium before a capacity crowd.

89. These walkers are really racing. You can see how stride length is achieved by swinging forward the front leg whilst the hip on the same side comes forward. The line of the creases in the athletes vests show this.

8.   INDOOR ATHLETICS

This is an area where there has been an expansion in athletics. It is a great spectator sport because no-one is too far away from the athletes and it makes all the year round competition possible. There is a boarded indoor track at RAF Cosford with banked curves. It is used regularly for competition and training in the Midlands and National and International competitions are held there.

It needs practice and judgement to run well on boards which are slightly springy. Instead of four bends in a 400 metres race the runners have eight, whilst the 200 metres men have four to negotiate instead of two on the normal track.

In the sprint, therefore, the best policy is to get to the front first in order to find out where the springy boards are, to wear needle spikes and get in the inside lane straight away.

For the longer distance races the finishing burst must come two laps from home so that the front position is gained before the last lap starts.

The bends are banked to compensate for their sharpness and the straights are so short that passing on bends is inevitable.

The importance of a good start is highlighted particularly in the 60 metre events.

Note how the measurements are in metres. This is how all tracks are being measured and laid out and most races are now measured in metres, as are the throwing and jumping distances.

90. The photograph shows Rodney Morrod of Birmingham University competing there. Note the special indoor shoes fitted with needle spikes and built to take the shock of hard take-off and landing. Weights on the hurdles give them the correct resistance to the hurdler, should he hit them and they prevent the hurdles from being toppled over too easily (as stipulated in AAAs rules)

91. *(top right)* Colin O'Neill of Westbury near Bristol has reached a high standard in 100, 220, 440 and 880 yds and 440 yds hurdles and long jump. He is a junior international and he is here competing indoors at Cosford. You should try as many events as possible
Note the boards about 1 ft wide, the banked track and the nearness of spectators

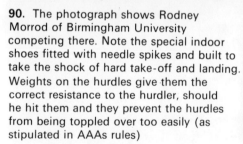

92. When you are speeding round the bends on the banked indoor track you can so easily go off course. Look at the inward lean. Now you can see why it is important to get to the bend first in an indoor sprint race

9. CHOOSING, USING AND LOOKING AFTER PERSONAL EQUIPMENT

TRAINING SHOES

You will certainly need a pair of these for use when you are warming-up, doing training runs and generally going about the track warming-up for competition or practising.

A number of good makes are available from sports shops so find a pair that fit well over a pair of socks. They are a better buy than gym shoes for athletic purposes.

SPIKED SHOES

These are a necessity in all outdoor athletics. For jumpers and hurdlers, spikes are needed in the heel as well as the sole of the shoe. Heel cups or rubber pads are often inserted to prevent bruising.

When you buy your spiked shoes make sure that they fit tightly over your bare feet, that the leather is fairly soft. Top class athletes often have their shoes made especially for them with yellow backed kangaroo skin uppers.

Different types of track, which range from grass to boards, need different spike lengths. For running on boards needle spikes which must be very fine and short are used whereas on a soft grass track $\frac{3}{4}$ in spikes can be used.

It is possible to buy shoes with interchangeable spikes. You should have two pairs of spikes one for competitions and a second pair for training in.

Since spiked shoes fit tightly you ought to use French Chalk or dusting powder so that your foot slips in easily and doesn't chafe. Don't stretch your spikes by pulling them off without untying the laces, and when you put them on push the toes right in before slipping on the heel. Some athletes wear chamois leather toe socks if there is chafing of the toes.

Shoes should be kept clean and dry and treated with care.

TRACK SUIT

This is another important item of clothing which you will use when warming-up and during training sessions.

Track suits come in all colours, shapes, sizes and materials.

A good first buy would be a cotton fleecy lined one, then later on a nylon one in your club colours will last you years. Some athletes prefer suits with more wool in them, though a sweater can be worn underneath any type of track suit in colder weather.

OTHER ITEMS

You will also need a holdall of some sort as, beside your singlet, shorts, spikes, training shoes, towel, and dusting powder, you might wish to have a stop watch and tape handy, together with a piece of string. This string can be marked with paint or have knots at appropriate points so that run-ups and check marks and take-off points can be readily laid down by simply unrolling the string and finding your markings or knots.

Keep all your kit clean and tidy, especially your track suit.

For the throwing events you need a cloth or rag to wipe your implement on wet days. Some discus throwers like to have slightly tacky hands so, like pole vaulters, they use Venetian turpentine. Hammer throwers use a leather glove which must allow the fingers to protrude, as with a mitten, and, like all the throwers, choose their footwear carefully.

10. FITNESS AND TESTING

In any athletic event the following qualities are required to a greater or a lesser degree:

1. Muscle strength
2. Endurance
3. Skill
4. Mobility.

The strength of muscles is used to move the weight of the body and limbs and, as with any 'engine', the lighter the load the easier it will be for the engine, or if the load stays the same but the engine is more powerful it will be easier for the engine. The load can be moved faster and this acts similarly to increasing weight.

We make it easier for our 'engines' by improving the quality of our muscle fibres so that we can move faster or more 'explosively'.

Strength acquisition is only part of the story. The ability to keep our body moving in sprinting or do many 'explosive' movements in jumping without tiring in the muscles before our opponents do is called muscle endurance. Individual muscle groups can tire without the body generally tiring. We don't get out of breath. This sort of endurance is called local muscle endurance.

Another sort of endurance we need is that which enables us to keep going for a long time without having to stop to get our breath. This is general endurance and is concerned with us having a good blood supply, a good heart pump, and efficient lungs for taking in and breathing out air. General endurance is particularly necessary to middle distance runners.

As we grow, and we gain experience, as we practise and take part in athletics so we become better. Difficult movements become easier, we can attempt different ones and we gain control over our movements.

Gradually we may not even have to think about some of the movements. We are becoming more skilful.

Next, in order to make our limbs go through a wider range of move-movements at the joints, we have to become more supple muscularly and to cultivate ligaments and tendons which allow 'looseness' in joints. This is mobility.

Strength, endurance, mobility and skill will all be developed at first merely by taking part in athletic activities provided that they are done continuously over a period and fairly regularly.

The essential thing in acquiring any physical effect is to take part, and to do the activity so that there is some sort of overloading. It is the variations in the methods used for creating overload which give us varied training programmes.

Strength can be acquired by weight training. While use of weights is recommended it should be emphasised that indiscriminate use of them can be dangerous and involve people in accidents, so certain safety precautions must be taken. These are listed below.

Basically an activity or exercise is repeated a number of times and this number of 'reps' is repeated as a group a number of times, this is a *set* of *repetitions* and high poundages produce strength most rapidly, that is to say, a few repetitions with heavy weights is more effective than the reverse.

The ultimate heavy weight is an immovable object and some athletes and strength trainers believe in trying to do just that. A typical exercise of this type is to use a doorway and try to push outwards at the uprights.

Here are some important things to remember when using weights:

1. Make sure that the collars on the bars are secure so that the weights do not come off.

2. Have someone standing by or use the stands with slides which are sometimes available.

3. Get the correct technique or you will rick your back or damage yourself through incorrect movements. Keep your head back when lifting, and your back straight.

4. Work different muscle groups in succession.

5. If you keep a record, and you should, then improvements can be seen. Knowledge of the results of your work will keep you going.

Here is a weight training schedule for a 16 year old jumper to *start* on—see Fig 14–15.

Warm-Up

Weight	Reps.	
20 lb	8	1. Squat jumping: weight behind neck.
5 lb	8	2. Abdominal curls: from lying on the back, head and chest only are raised holding a single weight behind head. Feet are fixed.
10 lb	8	3. Back raising: lie on the stomach and raise trunk holding weight behind neck, as above but prone.
10 lb	4	4. Single $\frac{1}{2}$ squat: single leg bending and stretching holding weight. Use the wall bars or rope in gym for support.
10 lb	8	5. Alternate arm press—dumbells: holding weights arms are stretched upwards alternately.

For muscle endurance increase repetitions with light weights.

For general endurance running of various forms is the best.

Forms of running not mentioned in this chapter are **interval running** in which the athlete runs full out for a set distance then recovers and repeats the run, **pyramid running** in which the athlete runs a gradually increasing distance with the corresponding amount of rest which increases as the length of run increases.

E.g.　　　　80 m with　80 m jog recovery
　　　　　　90 m with　90 m jog recovery
　　　　　　100 m with 100 m jog recovery etc.

Or　　　　　800 m with 800 m jog recovery
　　　　　　600 m with 600 m jog recovery
　　　　　　400 m with 400 m jog recovery etc.

This type of running will improve the ability to recover quickly after exercise and the ability to continue activity for longer periods.

jump

weight

feet fixed

Lying on the back.

Any exercises carried to the full range of the movement will maintain mobility and gymnastic exercises are useful in keeping the general mobility of joints.

The skill development as required for say sprint starting or triple jumping and comparable events can only come with the right practice. This is where a coach or sharp observer can help. Also the athlete must practise intelligently and thoughtfully so that he knows what he is doing, why mistakes were made and what movements he is performing. He who thinks before he practises improves best.

Repetition is absolutely necessary to acquire skill.

TESTING AND MEASURING

One way of finding out how strong you are is to measure the amount of muscle pull by using a dynamometer which gives you the amount of pull of particular groups of muscles, e.g. by gripping a grip dynamometer the hand grip can be measured.

Your leg strength or back strength can be measured on another type of dynamometer. Dynamometers are really adapted weighing machines. However, you can still tell that you are getting stronger without these machines by the increasing amount of weight you can lift.

Muscular endurance can be measured by the increase in the number of repetitions you can make of a particular exercise. For example by counting the number of pull-ups you can do when hanging by the hands and arms from a beam. Your ability to 'explode' (power) can be tested by doing standing long jumps and comparing results with previous trials. The improvement in heart and lungs can be tested by seeing how quickly your pulse drops after a series of step-ups on to a bench. This is called a Harvard Step Test, but the number of times you can run, say, 80 yds at your top speed with a minute's rest between is a good measure of your recovery ability. If you have kept a record of performances you will know you are improving when your number of repetitions goes up and the 80 yd time remains the same.

Here are some Jumping Scoring Tables for various activities worked out by Wilf Paish an AAA national coach. This selection is reproduced by his permission. They are power tests. These tables may be metricated by using the conversion tables on page 96.

Points	Standing Long Jump	Hop 25 yds secs.	Standing Triple Jump	5 Spring Jumps	Running 4 Hop & Jump	5 Stride Long Jump
100	12′ 3″	2·5	34′ 6″	56′ 0″	78′ 0″	23′ 11″
75	9′ 0″	4·2	28′ 3″	45′ 10″	63′ 9″	23′ 0″
50	6′ 11″	6·8	22′ 0″	36′ 0″	49′ 6″	17′ 0″
25	4′ 10″	8·0	15′ 9″	28′ 0″	37′ 6″	13′ 0″
1	2′ 0″	8·8	9′ 6″	20′ 0″	25′ 6″	7′ 0″

Activities are: (i) Standing Long Jump.
(ii) 25 yd Hop.
(iii) Standing Triple Jump.
(iv) 5 consecutive springs.
(v) Running 4 Hops and a jump.
(vi) 5 stride approach to Long Jump.

The figures given above are only a sample of the sort of thing which can be done. The top mark is that of a top class athlete, the bottom one that of a young novice. The in-between scores can be worked out proportionately, e.g. 3 ft 6 in for a Standing Long Jump would get 12 pts, 7 ft 11 in, 62 pts.

Some other tables using ten activities were published in 'Athletics Coach', March 1967, a AAAs magazine for coaches obtainable from AAAs Publications.

VERTICAL JUMP TEST

The vertical jump test is another simple way of measuring power. Here is a simple form of the test.

Stand facing a wall and with your heels on the ground and toes touching the wall reach as high as you can with arms outstretched and fingers pointed. No heel raising. Mark where the finger ends touch the wall.

Now turn and stand with your right side to the wall leaving just enough room for your arms to swing. Next gather yourself and without a rebound spring as high as you can. At the top of your flight when the arms are stretched upwards, turn the right arm and mark the wall as high up as you can with your finger tips (which should have been whitened or chalked so that they will make a mark).

The difference in distance between the lowest point and the highest indicates the actual height you have been able to lift yourself.

If you are springing over 20 inches you are doing reasonably well, below 17 inches means that you need to build up your power and 25 inches is excellent even though some international fully-trained men athletes reach 30 inches and over.

This testing and measuring of your power (spring), strength and endurance are not ends in themselves for athletes, but only a means of finding out more about yourself and your physical possibilities. Ultimately it is you and your previous best athletic performance, and you and your opponents in your particular event which count.

Whilst all this testing and measuring can be fun and knowledge of results can help, it is also the degree of determination to succeed, patient work, and understanding which will play a large part when the moment of active competition arrives.

Technique must be practised as physical fitness improves, and there is nothing like taking part in competitions with other athletes. There are some athletes who spend a lot of time doing athletic practices like pyramid running, interval running and weight training. They become good at these things and almost forget the event for which they are training. Competition in the actual events must be included in all training schedules.

Your event or events are special to you but be prepared to try other events sometimes, avoiding too early specialisation. By being determined to do everything even in training to the best of your ability you cannot but enjoy better athletics.

Metrication

Track distances are more often than not given in metres and so are distances jumped and thrown. In order to make these distances real and meaningful many of us have to convert metres and kilometres into miles, yards, feet and inches; that is to say, into imperial measure. Sometimes we want to convert the other way.

Here are some metric athletic distances converted to imperial measure:

Race Distances

Metres	Yds	Ft	Ins	Metres	Yds	Ft	Ins
60	65	1	11	800	874	2	8
80	87	1	$5\frac{3}{4}$	1000	1093	1	10
100	109	1	1	1500	1640	1	4
110	120	0	11	2000	1 mile 427 yds		
200	218	2	2	3000	1 mile 1520 yds		
400	437	1	4	5000	3 miles 188 yds		
				10000	6 miles 376 yds		

Note: For a quick conversion of kilometres to miles divide the kms by 8 and multiply by 5.

Distances: Feet to Metres

Ins	Metres	Ft	Metres	Ft	Metres	Metres	Ft	Ins
1	0·025	1	0·30	20	6·00	1	3	$3\frac{1}{4}$
2	0·05	2	0·60	30	9·10	2	6	$6\frac{1}{2}$
3	0·076	3	0·90	40	12·20	3	9	10
4	0·102	4	1·22	50	15·20	4	13	1
5	0·127	5	1·52	100	30·50	5	16	5

Weights: Pounds and kilogrammes
or

lbs	lbs/kgs	kgs	lbs	lbs/kgs	kgs
2·20	1	0·45	13·23	6	2·72
4·41	2	0·91	15·43	7	3·18
6·61	3	1·36	17·64	8	3·63
8·82	4	1·81	19·84	9	4·08
11·02	4	2·27	22·05	10	4·54